POCKET BOOK OF
COMPASSION

First published in Great Britain 2019 by Trigger

Trigger is a trading style of Shaw Callaghan Ltd & Shaw Callaghan 23 USA, INC.

The Foundation Centre

Navigation House, 48 Millgate, Newark

Nottinghamshire NG24 4TS UK

www.triggerpublishing.com

Copyright © Trigger Publishing 2019

All rights reserved. No part of this publication may be reproduced, stored in a retrieval system, or transmitted in any form or by any means, electronic, mechanical, photocopying, recording or otherwise, without prior permission in writing from the publisher

British Library Cataloguing-in-Publication data

A CIP catalogue record for this book is available upon request from the British Library

ISBN: 978-1-78956-140-1

Trigger Publishing has asserted their right under the Copyright, Design and Patents Act 1988 to be identified as the author of this work

Cover design and typeset by Fusion Graphic Design Ltd.

Printed and bound in Dubai by Oriental Press

Paper from responsible sources

POCKET BOOK OF
COMPASSION

www.triggerpublishing.com

INTRODUCTION

Modern life can be filled with so much: from the daily commute, a hectic schedule, cooking an evening meal; to those crucial turning points: quitting your job, moving house, finding love. Between the noise, it can be hard to find those all-important moments of quiet.

The Pocket Book of Compassion offers a little guidance for when the scales of life are tipped, times become turbulent and a moment of stillness is needed. From the minds of some of the world's most well-known figures, learn to find your footing, take a breath and stand on stable ground once more.

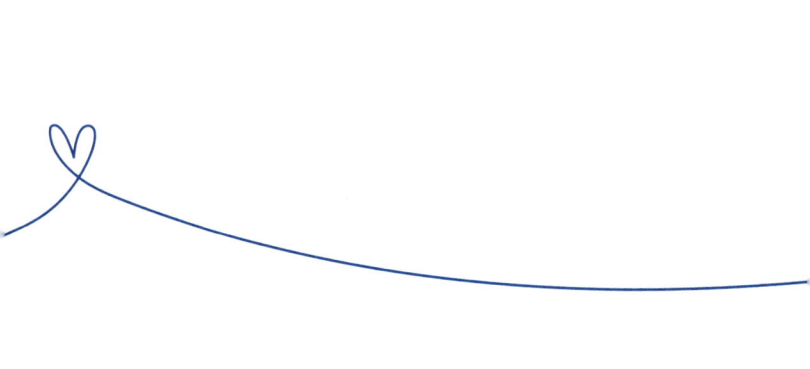

It doesn't matter who you are,
where you come from;
the ability to triumph begins
with you – always

Oprah Winfrey

Real living is living for others

Bruce Lee

Be good to yourself 'cause nobody else has the power to make you happy

George Michael

This planet is for everyone;
borders are for no one.
It's all about freedom

Benjamin Zephaniah

I tell my students, 'When you get these jobs that you have been so brilliantly trained for, just remember that your real job is that if you are free, you need to free somebody else ...

… If you have some power, then your
job is to empower somebody else.
This is not just a grab-bag candy game'

Toni Morrison

Do not judge me by my successes,
judge me by how many times
I fell down and got back up again

Nelson Mandela

... You'd be surprised
how far that gets you

Neil deGrasse Tyson

When you like someone,
you like them in spite of their faults.
When you love someone,
you love them with their faults

Hermann Hesse

To love is to recognize
yourself in another

Eckhart Tolle

Be kind, for everyone you meet
is fighting a hard battle

Plato

What's important is to
be able to see yourself, I think,
as having commonality with other
people and not determine,
because of your good luck ...

... that everybody is less significant,
less interesting, less important
than you are

Harrison Ford

Every life deserves a certain
amount of dignity, no matter how poor
or damaged the shell that carries it

Rick Bragg

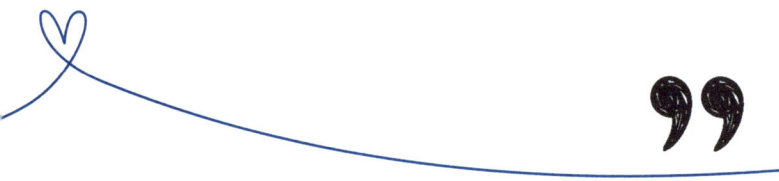

There is no exercise better
for the heart than reaching down
and lifting people up

John Holmes

Love and compassion are necessities,
not luxuries. Without them,
humanity cannot survive

Dalai Lama

We never know the journey another person has walked, so be kind to everyone

Lynette Mather

Someone I once loved gave me a
box full of darkness. It took me years to
understand that this, too, was a gift

Mary Oliver

That's what I consider true generosity:
You give your all, and yet you always
feel as if it costs you nothing

Simone de Beauvoir

Beauty is not who you are on the outside,
it is the wisdom and time you gave away to
save another struggling soul like you

Shannon L. Alder

One of the most spiritual things you can do is embrace your humanity. Connect with those around you today. Say, 'I love you', 'I'm sorry', 'I appreciate you', 'I'm proud of you' ...

... whatever you're feeling.
Send random texts, write a cute note,
embrace your truth and share it

Steve Maraboli

If a man cannot understand
the beauty of life, it is probably because life
never understood the beauty in him

Criss Jami

Both men and women should
feel free to be sensitive.
Both men and women should
feel free to be strong

Emma Watson

I speak to everyone in the same way,
whether he is the garbage man or
the president of the university

Albert Einstein

We may have all come on different ships, but we're in the same boat now

Martin Luther King Jr.

Whatever the present
moment contains, accept it
as if you had chosen it

Eckhart Tolle

No act of kindness,
no matter how small,
is ever wasted

Aesop

Every day, you have the power
to choose our better history by opening
your hearts and minds, by speaking up
for what you know is right

Michelle Obama

I know what I can do,
so I never doubt myself

Usain Bolt

Mistakes are always forgivable,
if one has the courage to admit them

Bruce Lee

Society's punishments are small compared to the wounds we inflict on our soul ...

... when we look the other way

Martin Luther King Jr.

You can't let your failures define you.
You have to let your failures teach you

Barack Obama

Everybody is a genius.
But if you judge a fish by its ability
to climb a tree, it will live its whole life
believing that it is stupid

Albert Einstein

If a person seems wicked,
do not cast him away.
Awaken him with your words,
elevate him with your deeds,
repay his injury with your kindness ...

... Do not cast him away;
cast away his wickedness

Lao-Tzu

Give the ones you love wings to fly,
roots to come back, and reasons to stay

Dalai Lama

There's only one of you,
so why would you want to look
like everyone else? Why would you
want to have the same ...

... hairstyle as everyone else
and have the same opinions
as everybody else?

Adele

I feel like if you're a really
good human being, you can try to find
something beautiful in every
single person, no matter what

Lady Gaga

Eventually you just have to realize
that you're living for an audience of one.
I'm not here for anyone else's approval

Pamela Anderson

Forgiveness liberates the soul.
It removes fear. That is why it is
such a powerful weapon

Nelson Mandela

You have this one life.
How do you wanna spend it?
Apologising? Regretting? Questioning?
Hating yourself? Dieting?
Running after people who don't see you?
Be brave. Believe in yourself …

... Do what feels good.
Take risks. You have this one life.
Make yourself proud

Cara Delevigne

Forgiveness is not an occasional act;
it is a constant attitude

Martin Luther King Jr.

Often, it is the most deserving
people who cannot help loving those
who destroy them

Herman Hesse

You deserve the best, the very best, because you are one of the few people in this lousy world who are honest to themselves, and that is the only thing that really counts

Frida Khalo

No one is born hating another person
because of the color of his skin,
or his background, or his religion.
People must learn to hate,
and if they can learn to hate ...

... they can be taught to love,
for love comes more naturally
to the human heart than its opposite

Nelson Mandela

I've been angry.
I've been incredibly angry and hurt.
But I've come to realise that I'm
not defined by my scars, but by the
incredible ability to heal ...

... and forgiveness is part of healing

Lemn Sissay

I have my flaws, but I embrace them
and I love them because they're mine

Winnie Harlow

Success is liking yourself,
liking what you do,
and liking how you do it

Maya Angelou

You need to be aware of what others are doing, applaud their efforts, acknowledge their successes and encourage them in their pursuits ...

... When we all help one another,
everybody wins

Jim Stovall

Art is to console those
who are broken by life

Vincent Van Gogh

When a person realizes he has been deeply heard, his eyes moisten. I think in some real sense he is weeping for joy.
It is as though he were saying ...

... "Thank God, somebody heard me. Someone knows what it's like to be me"

Carl R. Rogers

The hardest thing for not only an artist
but for anybody to do is look themselves
in the mirror and acknowledge,
you know, their own flaws and fears ...

... and imperfections and
put them out there in the open
for people to relate to it

Kendrick Lamar

Let no one ever come to you
without leaving happier

Mother Teresa

You're only given a
little spark of madness.
You mustn't lose it

Robin Williams

Desperation is a necessary ingredient
to learning anything, or creating anything.
Period. If you ain't desperate at some
point, you ain't interesting

Jim Carrey

It's difficult to believe in yourself
because the idea of self is an artificial
construction. You are, in fact, part
of the glorious oneness of the universe ...

... Everything beautiful in the world is within you

Russell Brand

Kind words can be short and easy to speak,
but their echoes are truly endless

Mother Teresa

I always just thought if you see somebody without a smile, give 'em yours!

Dolly Parton

There are things in my life that are hard to reconcile, like divorce. Sometimes it is very difficult to make sense of how it could possibly happen. Laying blame is so easy ...

... I don't have time for hate or negativity in my life. There's no room for it

Reese Witherspoon

You define beauty yourself,
society doesn't define your beauty

Lady Gaga

Talent wins games,
but teamwork and intelligence
win championships

Michael Jordan

Hating people because of
their color is wrong. And it doesn't
matter which color does the hating.
It's just plain wrong

Muhammad Ali

Weakness is something we don't like
to admit we have. We hold it against people,
until we experience it, and then we
feel more compassion for it

Olivia Wilde

Why would anyone want to be called
a size zero or even aspire to being a zero?
I don't even't understand the thinking
behind it, let alone the practicalities.
What is all that about?

Dawn French

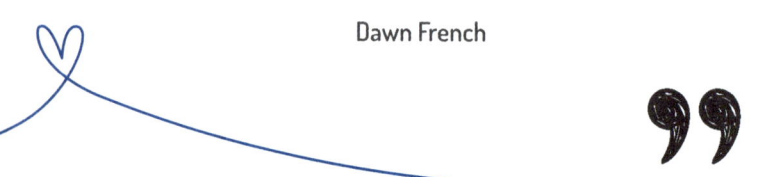

Everybody can be great …
because anybody can serve.
You don't have to have a college degree
to serve. You don't have to make
your subject and verb agree to serve …

... You only need a heart full of grace.
A soul generated by love

Martin Luther King Jr.

I used to think that confidence came
from what other people thought about me
but now I realize it comes from what
I feel about myself

Demi Lovato

There's nothing better than a
world where everybody's just trying to
make each other laugh

Matthew Perry

For me, success is a state of mind.
I feel like success isn't about
conquering something; it's
being happy with who you are

Britney Spears

Love is the most powerful force in the universe and we have the extraordinary ability to give and receive it

Tim A. Ewell

I think love is unconditional;
you find someone that you can grow
with and that makes you want to
grow and makes you a better person

Channing Tatum

None of us is as smart as all of us

Ken Blanchard

There is no such thing
as a self-made man.
You will reach your goals
only with the help of others

George Shinn

The gentle and sensitive companionship
of an empathic stance ... provides
illumination and healing. In such situations
deep understanding is ...

... I believe, the most precious gift
one can give to another

Carl R. Rogers

You know it's love when all you want
is that person to be happy, even if you're
not part of their happiness

Julia Roberts

There's nothing greater in the world
than when somebody on the team does
something good, and everybody gathers
around to pat him on the back

Billy Martin

Our primary purpose is to help others.
And if you can't help them,
at least don't hurt them

Dalai Lama

All the adversity I've had in my life, all my troubles and obstacles, have strengthened me ... You may not realize it when it happens ...

... but a kick in the teeth may be the best thing in the world for you

Walt Disney

You deserve a lover who listens
when you sing, who supports
you when you feel shame and
respects your freedom

Frida Khalo

Carry out a random act of kindness,
with no expectation of reward, safe
in the knowledge that one day someone
might do the same for you

Princess Diana

Your need for acceptance can
make you invisible in this world. Don't let
anything stand in the way of
the light that shines through this form ...

... Risk being seen in all of your glory

Jim Carrey

More smiling, less worrying.
More compassion, less judgment.
More blessed, less stressed …

... More love, less hate

Roy T. Bennet

Save one-third, live on one-third,
and give away one-third

Angelina Jolie

Empathy for other people's feelings requires
a counter-balancing quality of toughness
to not be controlled by their pain

Al Siebert

Love and kindness are never wasted.
They always make a difference.
They bless the one who receives them,
and they bless you, the giver

Barbara De Angelis

Instead of looking in the mirror
and focusing on your flaws,
look in the mirror and appreciate
your best features. Everyone has them

Demi Lovato

Strong people don't put others down.
They lift them up

Michael P. Watson

If your compassion does not
include yourself, it is incomplete

Jack Kornfield

I don't want to have plastic surgery.
I'm going to look like this forever.
Deal with it ...

... Once you deal with it,
you feel more calm about it

Adele

Being deeply loved by someone
gives you strength, while loving someone
deeply gives you courage

Lao Tzu

It is good to love many things,
for therein lies the true strength, and
whosoever loves much performs much ...

... and can accomplish much, and what is done in love is well done

Vincent Van Gogh

I'm not perfect ... But I'm enough

Carl R. Rogers

Tall, curvy, short, thin, whatever you are, you are beautiful

Demi Lovato

At the end of the day,
we can endure much more than
we think we can

Frida Khalo

When the other person is hurting, confused, troubled, anxious, alienated, terrified; or when he or she is doubtful of self-worth ...

... uncertain as to identity,
then understanding is called for

Carl R. Rogers

Nothing would mean anything if
I didn't live a life of use to others

Angelina Jolie

You cannot do kindness too soon,
for you never know how soon
it will be too late

Ralph Waldo Emerson

Remember there's no such thing
as a small act of kindness. Every act creates
a ripple with no logical end

Scott Adams

It's gonna be okay.
No matter how hard rock bottom is,
you can rise above it and
you can come back

Demi Lovato

A part of kindness consists in loving people more than they deserve

Joseph Joubert

Highly sensitive people are too often
perceived as weaklings or damaged goods.
To feel intensely is not a symptom
of weakness ...

... it is the trademark of the truly
alive and compassionate

Anthon St. Maarten

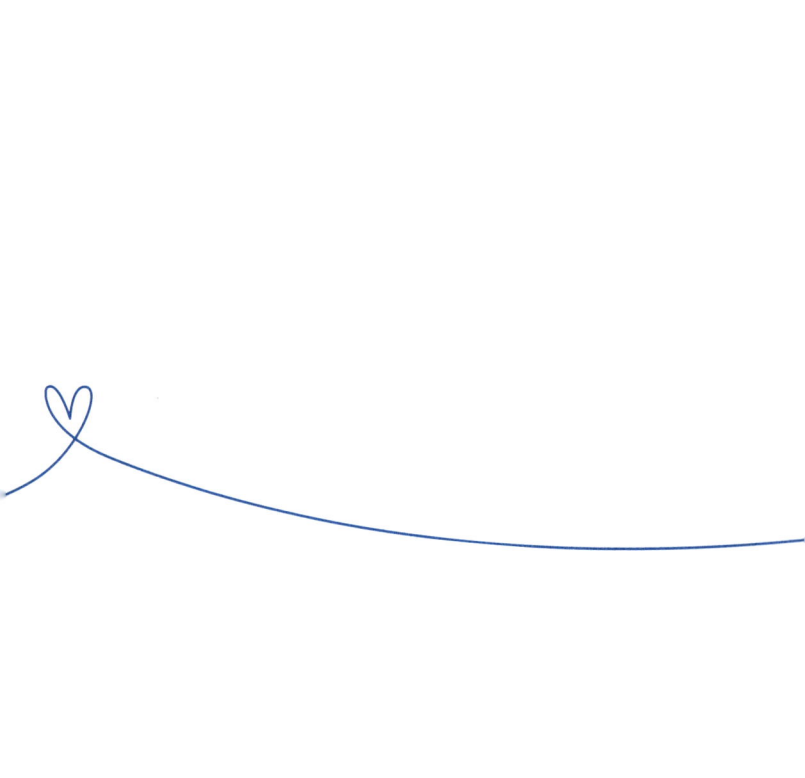

For a little guidance elsewhere ...

POCKET BOOK OF
RESILIENCE

For when life gets a little tough

POCKET BOOK OF
WISDOM

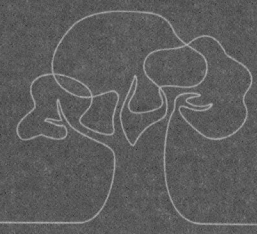

For when life gets a little tough

POCKET BOOK OF
BALANCE

For when life gets a little tough

www.triggerpublishing.com

Trigger is a publishing house devoted to opening conversations about mental health. We tell the stories of people who have suffered from mental illnesses and recovered, so that others may learn from them.

www.shawmindfoundation.org

We aim to end the suffering and despair caused by mental health issues. Our goal is to make help and support available for every single person in society, from all walks of life. We will never stop offering hope. These are our promises.